Echoes of the Rebellious Mind: Poetic Expressions

Poetic Perspective of Life Circumstances by a Mental Health Professional

BY
JIGYASA TANDON

BlueRose ONE
Stories Matter

First Published in February 2023

ISBN: 978-93-5704-267-3

BLUEROSE PUBLISHERS

www.BlueRoseONE.com

info@bluerosepublishers.com

+91 8882 898 898

Cover Design:

Jigyasa Tandon

Distributed by: BlueRose, Amazon, Flipkart

I would like to dedicate this book to Mr. Thomas Phillips, a Mentor to me, myorganization and a great friend to my father. It was a destiny to meet him and a pain to lose him. However, whatever time I have spent with him has been exceptionally motivating and enlightening. Thanking him for the tremendous impact he has had on me as a writer, I wish to dedicate this book to the first reader of my poems, my very own Thomas Uncle.

Foreword

"Traveller, there is no road; you make your own path as you walk."

This famous Spanish proverb comes to my mind as I read the sublime verses penned by Jigyasa Tandon compiled in her book "Echoes of the Rebellious Mind".

The poems have a common thread, depicting resilience and enormous inner strength to navigate through turbulent tides, that we all experience in our lives, especially through our free-flowing emotions and a parallel line of constant interferences and conflicts auto produced by our mind.

Most of us with our innocence, sensitivity, behavioural flexibility and a knack to adjust in adversities, find happiness in a myriad of situations, eventually emerging triumphant.

Jigyasa Tandon, having rich experience in dealing with mental health issues, in these poems seamlessly blends contradictions of life with impeccable solutions, by searching her inner subconsciousness.

She has painted a delicate canvas of emotions, using a variety of shades, from her colour palette of experiences, representing uncanny feelings towards growing up and interactions with different social settings.

This book epitomizes what a human consciousness is capable of. Her poems manifest courage to overcome the harsh realities of life, while simultaneously taking a journey of self-discovery, without losing faith in self or the phenomenon of human existence.

I wish Jigyasa a huge success in life and wish she continues to pen her experiences and publish the same for the benefit of her readers, friends and admirers.

Mr. Sanjay Jain

Additional Solicitor General of India
(Supreme Court)
Government of India
New Delhi

Preface

On A Certain Day, when I look at the sky, I ask, 'What do I see?' On A certain day, when I look at the land, I ask, 'what do I see?'

On A certain day, when I look at the flowing water, I ask, 'what do Isee?'

Gradually, with every passing day, I questioned everything, what do I see, And Finally, the miracle happened, I found the answer, which satisfiedme-

I see not what I see, I see what you, they and we want you to see.

Life is similar to child's play. Ironically it can be as simple as a click of a finger or can be as tough as struggling to become someone. The underlined motto remains the same, the better we know, the better we understand. In the end, it's all about how well we are versed with the rules and how much did we practice.

While initiating this book, my mind was cluttered and tormented with questions of lowering self-worth, confusion, and fears of unbeaten failures. I felt hopeless and helpless thinking about the future and tired with the work I was doing then. I felt directionless, overwhelmed and nowhere to head.

Everybody shared their piece of expertise with me on several such instances. The option was logically in place but jumping on the path was a little difficult. I, like most others, evaluated the outcomes and focused upon the ways those outcomes were to be achieved, how others were heading towards that direction and maybe replicating those actions would reap the same benefits for me. However, by simply deciphering replicating those actions and behaviours didn't pay off that well. I felt more detached from myself. I observed that my actions simply did not have any heart into it, no manifestation of self into it. That's when I decided, that this is not the right path for me. I would challenge, I would focus on change, I would deduce my own methodology and chart out my own path to my destiny, and in turn would encourage the same behaviour. This has set the tone for my opinion on life, which says that, things will go on in the manner which has been assertively suggested to you, but if you really want to feel the change, you have to make attempts towards it.

My Journey of Writing

In my phase of utter dullness, I made many attempts to chalk out ways that could offer me moments of rejuvenation among the chaos. Finally, I crafted out the method which helped me explore an altogether new side to me and laid out possibilities that I thought never existed.

In my course of action, I began with *Mission Walks*. The thumb rule that had to be followed was that I had to compulsory move out of the four walls of my house and walk around the city while observing the big and small nuances of the mundane life. Sounds quite simple, right? But here's the trick, I had to click a picture and describe about it, what and how it made me feel, what that picture meant to me. – What ignited me to take the picture, what that fire meant, and where was it directed.? After a few failed trials, I started developing an interest in it. In this process, it came to my realization how one locked moment can have a bunch of unlocked meaning meanings within it, and how it is upto the author and observer what interpretation one can make out of it.

After getting a hang of it and becoming comfortable with it, I started blogging on the same concept. I termed it picture- quotes format.

Under the pen name of ***"roadsidestoryteller"***, I initiated my Instagram and WordPress blog. Around this time, I came across the concept of spoken - word poetry. The whole idea of it was quite encouraging and proved to be supplementing to my original idea. Now, the next thing I knew was I was writing poetry on the pictures I took. This itself was a lot satisfying and it could say things loud that my feelings and words together couldn't express. Along with this, life had other share of things which kept happening. But whether it was a lovely moment or hardship period, my attitude towards them started to change. I focused on finding a way not following an expected path.

In nutshell, it just about 3 things: *intention, perception and action*. If you have a good heart, you'll view things beautifully and hence act with gratitude not attitude. Thus, keep it simple silly!

Jigyasa Tandon

Acknowledgments

DASTAK SE DASTAAN TAK

I would love to acknowledge the efforts of my father, Mr. Vivek Kumar Tandon, to make me what I am today and giving me the independence toexplore myself and encouraging me write my own career path.

I am extremely grateful to my mother, Ms. Mamta Tandon; my sister, Ms. PrernaTandon; and my partner, Mr. Sagar S Pandey. Without these people, my life is an empty shore. I like the waves, waves are constant, maybe the intensity of the waves change, but they remain a couple to the seashore.

Special mention of my Mami, Aradhana Ray Vermani; my Mamu, Bharat Vermani; and my youngest brother, Ivaan Vermani for being a good sport to my 3 am crazy ideas and being there throughout the ups and downs of my journey.

Contents

Section One

Mental Health: A Familiar Inner Connection

The 'I'

When I walk towards you,
I picture a hundred possibilities

A hundred thousand struggles,
few humps, and multiple hurdles,

But for any visionary success,
This creates a balance,

Helping the greed sound reasonable
and the achievement feel 'well priced'.

Thus, when I walk back,
To life,
I see,

Praises being thrown at me randomly,
Making the applause feel less believable
And acceptance in difference, more truthful

A captured feeling to live freely takes a new birth,
This time with an intention to stay and strive,

To be grounded with roots
Healthy and strong
Pulling together strings
Of gold and silver,

Creating a definition for
A beautiful lining called 'I'.

Depression: A Living Experience

Sitting in a closed room
Watching over the walls
I go blank with blues around

The chaos the silence offers
Is imitated by the hovering darkness
Captivated, suffocated
I ask the forces to let go
Let the sunrise fall over
And not just behold the sunset

But… nothing happens
I shout to nothing but vacuum
The mellow night takes pride
Over the time, the energy is lost

All I can find scattered shattered pieces of my soul
With anything refusing to putting it together and filling the wound.
The casting shadow takes away everything,
Just leaving a mere skeleton
With depressed emotions.

Set aside are the onlookers of sadness, dancing and singing in pride
Don't come near me or you'll to get infected
Maybe... I am not vibe you want around

In the market of worldly materials, I might be bought, sold or acquired
But never will I be befriended
Than by lies, sorrows, and despair

Run away, it is the only solution.

Beauty of Variance

When the beauty of variance of colours begin to crawl
into your life,
splashing around the blot of colour embarking
bondage and binds,
it's time of realisation that
life isn't constant with its phases,

Ups and downs, lefts and rights, all chain up together
like studs in anecklace,
Changes happen, page by page,
With scribbled notes and fill-in pictures
designing situations
Convincing us with the convenience
of time and space,
Allowing us to be both shy and Loud
within a life frame,

All we are left with is to define Strokes and add spice,
Sprinkling glitter, or varnishing the painting in pride.

Ring of Uncertainty

The turmoil was stiff
It hardened the soul
Inside out, the situation was vague
And uncertain,

Stuck between the choice and chance
Everything stood risky
Like a hedge hanging on the edge of the building
A little hope was there, deep within, somewhere

But it fluttered,
Giving shades of darkness
Blinding my strength in phases,
The train seemed to run in the opposite directions
The destination seemed an unusual decision
Situations slipping one by one,

It ached...
But it wasn't solution,
A question kept popping throughout
Was this my chance of
Working towards acceptance of doubt?

Delusional Living

On A Certain Day, when I look at the sky, I ask, 'What do I see?'
On A certain day, when I look at the land, I ask, 'what do I see?'
On A certain day, when I look at the flowing water, I ask, 'what do I see?'

Gradually, with every passing day,
I questioned everything, what do I see,

And then, the miracle happened,
I found the answer, which satisfied me...

I see not what I see, I see what you, they, and we want you to see.

The Blue

It took me time to sink in,
What each shade of colour blue meant,
For at first, I had laid my foundation
as a common man,
That blue was the ray of hope
that brightened the sky,
But sipping through the tea of gloomy existence
Reading between lines was the habit I picked,
Leading to nothingness and blank slates,
Readily waiting to be Redecorated every minute
With coloured chalks and hidden meanings,
Tangled much within the mingled world,
Safety and security were something I questioned first
But to my understanding, it lit the wrong fire causing
danger and harm,
With each darkened chapter, the silence of taboos
broke
Confronting the challenges and artificial love
that surrounded it.

The Inky Sky-Space

I sat in lap thinking it'll offer calmness
Least I knew what I was challenging myself do
He offered me to sit in water puddle
It felt special , cool and warm, side by side
It reflected colours I couldn't define
It was wrapped in wind of mesmerising exchange of words,

As it furthered, the weather darkened
It was neither warm, neither cold,
Neither it reflected colours of love.
The water changed itself to its muddy self
I was too was stiffening, becoming loveless
I felt like dead in the living world
Distance increased from the normality
My happy picture was just left as a cutout on the table

The force became stronger, inexpressible
I fought the battle but alas, I lost
I was left muddled with all the dirt around
I was exhausted yet questioned
Is this what friendship all about?

Does it involve breaking the other to an extend?
The inky sky spread everywhere
The stars weren't illuminated anymore
There eyes seemed closed
With lost trust in me and

Plea for Peace: A Restoration of Balance

His hollow eyes looked past me
Like a skeleton didn't exist within
It was only a mass filled body
Which he wished to cut in pieces,
Roast and eat away to glory,
It didn't matter to him that how grey I was
How my existence made the world strive.

For him, he was an extremely qualified
Professional by the structure,
His scarified sleeps, motherly cuddling
And family of situations of fun,

Connection and communication had
Burned multiple holes in his heart,
Leaving him halfway through development,
Forming a scary depression of revenge and revolt.

In between series of twists, licks and lucks
He learnt the trade and understood the trademark

And cracked the code by drawing strings
With baits of needs, desires and desperation
Giving him undefinable strength and
Internalising a wolf in him,

A stare guided you to a home of
Fear, control and rough marksmanship
The home looked brightly light and
Beautiful from a distance
Shining in shallow glory and fancies
A strong black and white look to a perfect shoreline.

To a great dismay, people forget how glorious things
Speak a one-sided story and too much fancy lights
Leave you blinded with aching and a blurry eyesight

Within the house,
All by his wish, a model was in place,
Tables were arranged in a dictated manner,
Choice was just an apparent show,
Compulsion was a mere by-product

A dictionary with a reference code of influence
Ensured the vocabulary to be limited and mudding of
every opened loop that muddle arguments,
For he induced a mental conviction of power that he
scribbled everywhere

Escaping was my method, gene by gene,
Generation by generation,
It was affirmed more and more of,
But how many times could survival be assured by this

Thus, I wrote about reform through a vociferous
stance of language and actions,
It stumbled him and he didn't know what to do,
like a jitterbug walking through lanes of shaken
reality

As he was familiar that it'll spike offenders and
define support against his ways,
A march of assemblyman would definitely demand
throwing him out of power,
Restoring archaic ways that seemed incredibly
upsetting and stupid

As he lacked the experience of what failing, falling,
belonging and rising looked like,
It was all taken away from him and
He was urged with force to follow linearity,
dismissing the natural earthly bipolarity

But now, it was not an option but an affirmation,
I had to learn the other side of the trade,
A secret that was kept away or was mispronounced by
many wayward people

And controllers like him helped them believe that
What they were doing was right and weakened them by
Using language of threat and punishments,
Conditional motivational-acceptance as you may call it

Now, pleasingly peace would love to
Find an opportunity to redefine, rehab,
Reform and re-lay ships of communication,
Righteous information and progressive education
And rarely accessible yet sacred principles of mental
healthcare system in regards to the comfortable
environment of possible physical phoning behaviours

Strengthening Yourself

Just when you think,
Things aren't on the right path,
The feeling of being scattered hovers,
You feel all broken and distributed,
Time of fall seems nearer,
It allows you to feel you are unable to be you,
Stop and think
Say this to yourself,
Life is testing your comfort,
Making you think and wonder
You might feel weak,
But it's the strength you are building,
You'll explore the side of you,
You never thought you own,
Don't let yourself down with labels,
Liberalising the spirit will feel more internalising,
Regard yourself with beauty of the understanding of the unknown,
Don't ever put boundaries and limit your abilities,

You are the Power,
You are the Abundance.
Love yourself, Accept yourself.
The Victory will be in your court, therein.

Counselling: A Path to Recovery

It was a white empty room
It had some structures
With the office usuals
And a room with only two people in it
Her and me, across the table

The emptiness of the room reflected in me,
While I sat in silence shouting at me
Preparing myself to recycle the moment
To reproduce in front of her
And take the discussion further
Over and over through the sessions

She expected me stiff
While I expressed my emotional narrative
That difficult morning, I told you about the other day,
Where, I lost nothing, but myself
In the process of ripping away

I told her more and more,
In the beginning, it felt, it led me somewhere

I was nothing more and nothing less than
A mere skeleton of facts and body movements
It left me losing power of emoting and thinking

The saga of sessions took over a period of time
The chronicle of back and forth of doubt
The struggle to claim clarity continued
I firmly sang my song of what happened
Like a tale from the moral book

She made her judgement about my disease, I couldn't tell,
At places she felt the need to question my assumptions of the world
She told me to ponder,
Was it all imagined or a fabricated story
Or a real incident took place to solidify the stance
To which I zoned into blankness
The time flashed in front
And it felt sitting there in front of incident like a movie
Where it ran all again, like 9-12 dailies

The clock danced in front of her,
I had my head hanging down like forever
The comforting, warm hug
Of depression felt so powerful
And I failed to answer

My heart wanted to regress into a child of age 2
Where I could just cry, cry and cry it all out
To just express that I wasn't okay
I wanted undying attention
To save from harm inflicted inwards
As I was losing worth to live

She stopped me once, then
Asked me to think
To reflect on insight gained
She asked again
But this time, it was different from the first
She asked whether I was ashamed of what happened ?
She questioned was it my fault or his
I was muted,
But a slight nod expressed my stance

She confronted my inability to assess
And I told that how's the society tell
The fault lines are within me and
He's flying on some miraculous carpet of freedom

It took more than a while,
But as the time went by
I could see me moving
Forming, changing, thinking and emoting
Abilities, she mentioned,
I thought only existed under the rock of expectations

But conversing with her helped
Every week, those 45 minutes
Did something unusual,
While presumably it felt I was just talking over

I trusted someone in a while,
When everyone seemed away
She was the sun that shined
Counselling makes a difference is what I realised

As some months passed by
She became a friend with a distance
Filled with respect for the ethics
Now I tell this with pride,
I am heading a healthy road to recovery

Section Two

Women by her Counts

A Difficult Morning

Not all seemed well that morning,
I was on a swing, sitting still
Starring with hollow eyes
Without a blink to fill in the blank
In the zone of darkness and blackness
Whether it was a question or
An array of scattered thoughts

I still couldn't battle throughout
The pain was heavy this time,
It was not the mouth but the vaginal gap
That shouted for help, that shouted for love
That shouted for concern, that shouted for any voice

The morning seemed one with the sun
Rising to its maximum power,
And clouds with sudden streak
Winning the game of hide & seek
Leaving everything with greys anatomy
Or maybe a little more than it

Was it me or the air becoming windy,
I failed to decide,
Did I lose with the play or heroically made a score,
I failed again,
Against the decision-making supreme power,
Though, it kept saying that
Strength needs care,
Identity needs definition

What that night had brought
Wasn't a gift card from a shopping store
But a lifetime membership of
Something you could have never wished for
But salesmanship had its own manner
The magic worked and you get trapped

That morning brought me to a broken-down home
To a stray house with torn-apart clothes,
And scratches stretched across the body,
Fulfilling someone's wandering lust
And attempts to 'fix me' to the tag of coolness
As they laughed it out over drinks to pleasure

It wasn't a morning of sorts that's expected often,
But when we hear, tears roll down,
And we are left with nothing to offer
Barriers become more stringent
Strings to mental breakdown become prominent

And a promise to half burnt cigarettes
Are only ones made regularly to
Schedule a relationship between the I and you a little more comfortable....

But, you know,
How they say, promises are always meant to be broke?
What do you think happened to those?

A Wall That Speaks Volumes

I don't intimidate
Contrary to what people say,
They may be right or wrong,
But an experience of depth and height
Makes us realise what's beyond the world,
Inside out.

I speak truth to create the caricature,
Not mould myself to fit in
I carry a realisation that
I have the power to empower
And not feel empty and fearful.

If my words hurt, that's not much of a matter
What does, is the underlying mentality I am a woman,
I walk a path towards peace and equalization,
I am the wall, I speak volume.

A Questionable Identity

You'll try all your best to touch me,
Tease me, mock me or kiss me,
Putting all your efforts to please me.

If I give in to your request, you'll call me a variety,
And if I resist, I'll be an orthodox aunty.

If I step back, you make sure to pinpoint
To make me feel guilty,
If on other hand, I approach, you'll show me off
As just another feather added to your identity.

You'll confuse me, judge me, and
Fill me with negativity
But it is on me, will I be ready
No, I would answer to run away,
Yes, to let you find your way.

Oh Lord, help me on path so stray
Battle, conflict, sorrow, destruction
Or happiness, peace, success, satisfaction

I decide, to be firm, to be strong, be myself,
To shatter the pain, to move ahead
I praise myself,
For being a woman.

The Want

I want to escape, she said,

Away from this cynicism of the real world
Where my identity is considered more important
than my role,
Where my smile is preferred over my tears,
Where my dreams are looked upon more than my deeds.

To a place where I am what I am and not what they want
me to be.
I want to move away from my perception of monochrome
dreams.

Boundaries

In the bazaar of worldly materials
I might be sold, bought, and acquired
for my beauty or charisma,
But never will I be befriended
No one would lend their ear to listen
To my love, sorrow, or despair
Staying within the boundaries
is the only solution

A Warrior

I see you every day,
Making a commotion within chaos,
Like a lighthouse and rocks
Working without fail
Making efforts without a tear,
Upbringing a child without despair
Questioning your own morals
What's right and what's wrong
For my own born,
Your concern, this way,
makes me Respect you more,
Not denying the part you are my Superhero.
Don't lose one day my saddened face will be bright
again

Maybe faith is all you need,
maybe faith is all you need.

An Ode to a Mother

A melody found a home in her heart with my presence
Defining a destined relationship wrapped in emotions
And filling her blank page with scattered thoughts.
It was her chance to sculpt an artwork carefully
Reflecting her hard work, love, and creativity.
With every stanza of motherhood she wrote,
She brought aimlessly wandering words together in a rhythmic tone.
The lyrics of her unheard song seized her experiences
Of the unending journey of moulding and modulating.
On me, she inked her most beautiful poetry.

An Ode to a Teacher

As she entered,
She prepared a song
With her words woven into mesmerising sentences
Portrayed beautifully in the stanzas expressing and
sharing love, grace, and knowledge.

Through the song she sang,
She touched us with the lyrics of her course.

The tone of the melody varied from the twittering of
the birds to the ranting of rats.
Making us feel connected and motivated like ripples
in the standing water.

Her song deported me to the world of powered
thoughts and strong determination to serve others
In the flow of her song, she prepared her song to be
sung to the world through us.

The Literal Defiance

The trouble is paradoxical Indian society
It fails to affirm a formidable sentence
And calls it a paragraph of defective eyes
At every point a parent is questioned
For not able to design their human property nice
After a lot of baffling, I get it, I understand
The idea is to isolate from the isolation of the isolated
Ensuring maintenance of culture, as they like to say
Forgetting how we are left stranded in the challenged
rain of icy values and customs every time
Without cover, asking for help
But, ensuring help is pretentious
You wither and rust, when you call your cry
Staying away from away is all the protection you find
This settles for and settles by standing for community
The idea is they commune your ideas to be for one
Rejection of difference is the gifted almighty duty

Section Three

Life, It Builds, Step by Step

A Book called Life

The Journey appeared simple
All it showed was a path filled with happiness,
achievements, and success
But then promises happened
Some remained unfulfilled, some were broken
Some made shadows that never faded
With good times came the bad ones
Hurdles turned into lessons, flowers, and fruits into
blessings
Destiny became the best teacher
Death made us realise that end is inevitable
The Journey was travelled for years
But made it to one page to
the Book of the World, called Life.

Twinkle Twinkle, Little Stars

Just imagine...

What if the twinkle twinkle, little stars we often talked of during our childhood spoke a language through their twinkling?

What if they were telling us to stop imagining wonders or Dreams are lies that people spoke all the time?

What if they were telling us that life will be full of hurdles and struggles?
And we would be left with no option but to sail through them?

What if they were telling us that the brighter they shine they are trying to shout loud and tell us that we have a choice among the chaos?
The choice to struggle or draw a picture to learn a lesson?

What if they were telling us that darkness against which they are visible is nothing but an illusion like how they say is depression?

What if they were saying that emotions are bleak lines
like horizons and not all be encouraged on a surface
of humanitarian forces?

What if they were telling us that it's either way of the
coin you have to be to be accepted?
Living a four-dimensional life in a three-dimensional
world is merely possible.

What if they were saying that alone they are lonely
and nobody realizes their individual potential,
but it's only when they are together, they are realised
and loves for the shine they produced?

What if they were warning us that this dreaming
dream is to this day, the same people will force to
study them one day?

And then...
The truth will be nothing but the facts which you and
I have created together.

Last Shades of the Sun

It's a time that can be described as a recipe of humans dipped in traditionsand culture, norms and bonds, roles and status, and a struggle to fight forright with a pinch of nostalgia to garnish the dish that's served perfectly with a cup of 'chai' before everyone retires for dreamy nights.

Café Culture

Fairy lights, fancy couches, attractive air freshener,
vibrant atmosphere, and a big cup of coffee
A typical sight I come across in cafes located at every
nook and corner.

They say, they find it homely and comfortable.
Spending time to themselves and thinking of others.
Exertion finds it its rest and the soul finds its peace
While the owner counts his profits with a bill of
extreme GST.

*But, to my wonder, I often think, does this apparent spell
of warmth bring comfort to their shivering souls?*

Flipping the coin, what I often find,
The story penned has a moral of pretentious beings
Hiding their real sides to appear standing in the line.

Tired faces, drooping eyes, tightened shoulders,
And a bent body pose,
Carrying the weight of their souls shouting,
Screaming for love and acceptance,
To be looked after with care and support.

Making a simple plea
For letting them occupy space
At places of interest and responsibility,
And not to be simply termed as *rebels*.

A longing, not to enter their own homes
with feelings of distress.
To feel belonged and not to wander as a lonely cloud

The fear of judgements hovering over
Making us nothing more than mere zombies,
dreading and devoid of emotions.

Every heart, spells the same prayer.
Oh, buddy, please listen, I am afraid, I am being
vulnerable to distress and pain.
Sit with me, and share a smile.
I am a half burnt-out candle, light me, again.
Empower me, by being there.
Maybe I recover, and make a decision of living stays.

The deed of goodness is not conditioned for some.
We all are broken, held together with hope calming the
wounds.
Let's stand up and build an empire of strength.
It isn't impossible,
Only the fire of motivation needs to spread.

A Diary

As they open to the blank pages I offer
A mysterious smile widens
Illuminating their faces.

They enter the world of their own
Allowing a rare meeting with themselves
Happiness, despair, sorrow, love
All elements find their expression.

Writing down experiences caught up in the bottle
Making Peace with their soul and
Taking little steps towards serenity

I wish all their dreams and fantasies come true
With a hope that their words continue to pen on me,

As they open the blank pages I offer,
They open their hearts and let themselves be,
spilling all their truth on me,
Their Diary.

Questioning Choices

It's amazing to see how we all come to a point where to understand few things simply means feeling emotions that touches us in loving ways.

How, despite driving cars, it's a nostalgic picture of cycle that takes away the heart.
How, despite buying an ice cream overloaded with fancy toppings, it's a simple white softy that lures the heart away.
How, despite constant fighting for rights and responsibility, it's standing unitedly together that comforts us.
How, despite claiming variety in identity, it's being human what holds us together.
How, despite wishing for happiness all the time, experiencing tones of all the emotions helps keep us healthy.
How, despite dividing things between you and me, it's 'we' or 'us' that charms us better.

Humans: A definition

We humans are just earthly chaos living together,
Patterning, questioning, unlearning into uncountable and unaccountable experiences,
Designing and laying out our varied preferences and perspectives
What's more than given, less than taken,
It's all in one or one in all.

The Path

That path,
It marked some significance
Something mystic, it upheld
People had stories of all sorts
Describing, being afraid, entangled in myths.

Did it lead to some dark destiny?
Some agreed, some disagreed
It was all a paradoxical fantasy
Whoever went, returned different
denying the rule of the world
It was special in its own way.

Giving a thought,
I lead the path
Discovered a paradise, a life,
an aesthetic view
Something, everyone desire.
In that very moment
A simple lesson was derived.

Follow your heart,
Notions and perceptions of others,
Will always divide,
It’s all about a person, meaning, and a life.

A Machine called School

Empty corridors,
Silent classes,
Died creativity.

Making us travel
On the road most taken,
To prepare much prominence
The non-progressive machines.

Providing us no scope of failures
And no guarantee of a life of intact
principles giving way to success.

Leaving no choice to act with freedom and growth
Only pain of detained manufactured stock
Pushed on the path of unethical supplements
To make constant amends and corrections.

With high-ended expectations to
Deliver beyond held calibre and potential
But not to possibly ensure betterment
Letting humans become living beings

There is a need,
A need to break the vicious cycle of producing
Non-intrusive human machines
Embracing abstract beauty and confusion in thought
Supported with fresh air, human ailments and
development.

Section Four

Corona, An Unexpected Halt

Corona Anxiety: A Poetic Expression

You leave me
To sit alone with
known strangers called my family,
They know me since my birth, may be an year earlier,
But now the distance of running life have brought us to
a standstill

Now it's a state of incubation,
An emergency, where they'd rule, and we would
listen, Leaving us with dictated rule to abide by.
They say, state within, with them, the family during a
pandemic calling it a safe place
to rejoice for love and care.

But little you'd know,
This safety measure costs me more,
Thickening my skin and placing my guard
Are the steps followed in the need of the hour,
The stables of routine of saying low and less are
unbalanced, Truths laying in dangerously raw
situation

Ready to spill out for review, if caught
The pause is hovering over
Like examination blues.
Week by week, we have to stay together,
To close to understand each other, Getting on the drill,
Stone, scissors and roar
The peace is totally chucked out,

Still, with no choice left, silence is the key,
Which beholds us keenly,

Quiet, unknown, pretentiousness to its core
Managing too much in too little space,
Fireballs of forces together seem overwhelming and a struggle to deal with O Mankind, if you would have been kinder,
The world would have been better,
The star would shine twinkling with glitter,
Trees would grow, letting the lamps of hope illuminate a thousand home,

The machines would come but not compete with my father,
leaving my mother, no choice to cope with perfectionism of taste of greens and butter,
And if my brother wouldn't be their first preference and against whom I lost my lot of sisters,

And me happening to be their second child, about
whom they hardly bother,
Maybe then,
this quarantine would have been a little better,
Where I wouldn't have felt choked on Being cuddled
by my mother,
And questions from my father didn't pinch me like
injections, Filling me with disgust, hatred, and anger,
Leading me to feel emotional
And thoughts of suicide, death, and danger
To my side corner.

Wave Two, Ripples of Pain

I was happy. It was February.
Distress was low-key and functionalities had just started to get resolved.
Things started to look good. It helped me too!
By motivating me to get hold and move forward with a sense of sight and significance.

Then came March-end, and the structure started showing signs of disturbance.
Something was brewing up, we had anticipated the same,
But somewhere in our hearts and brain, we were acting pretentious to the idea that it'll be back
And lock us again in a quadrant of the small community I have called mine.
Things will restrict, and slow down and we'll have nothing but access to essentials merely.
That too with little money in the booklet challenging the whole life and its savings.
Tipsy turvy land and water were only to view but not excite,

Where land was captured with the virus, the water
lived with freedom from man's intervention.
April hits and crashes the structure altogether!
The system failed to ensure security, healthcare
services were experiencing a tornado of their own.
Rushing, crashing, falling, standing up again, doing
everything to sustain themselves,
and fetching resources from where they could.
Not knowing that resources may have the potential to
backfire too,
black fungus, diabetes, stress, anxiety, and depression
had become the new guests knocking at the door.

Come to the power, everyone went silent.
A part of them felt that it wasn't their chore to fetch
people from sinking mud.
They ensured religious liberty for their people by
facilitating the participation of dripping in water.
Ensuring their power in the right sector!
Where some initiated a blame game and fake cries.
Even the justice questioned the lack of rationality and
logic they called to empower with.
The battle had an expected result, dying people to
satisfy the egos of the powered individuals.
Life crisis, abandoned children, parents dealing with
the loss of young children.
Questing a chance to secure the future of their
counterparts.

Nothingness was only answering as a reply.
The situation started becoming better for the rest.
Education demonstrations began with hiking fees,
forced exams, and not considering pain and struggle.
A market of quacks and hoarders too began to set up!
With dead hope, only suspects were leftovers.

The Mental Health Battle

We always find ourselves in a battle field,
A battle to win or lose,
A battle in which emotions knock at our door
In which love writes twisting tales,
Falling apart, or coming together,
It's all about the various high and low points of the battle.
In this battle we can lose easily,
By not letting our being our ourselves
Following a pursuit that doesn't fits our body to its best,
Defining purposes of not being able too,
Disabling orientation of weakening within of the souls.
Not allowing emotions enter or leave,
Pursuing a life perfect like a robot,
Even if it drives away our body of all motion
To win is a simple understanding of struggle,
A less likely of what occurs,
In a zoom perfectionism it has to be all happy in reflection.

To win, is letting yourselves fall apart and gain strength from refraction of knowledge,
To win, is wavelength to survive from darkness to colour,
Not all have the prince with shining armour,
For some it's standing tall with wounds and scars with no one to cover,
To win, is to enable motion, live in and breathe little by little of freshening emotions.
Developing positive vibes, empowering drip by drip,
To win, will not happen in a day, it'll take time to learn and restore, your sleep and sores,
Then finally you'll strike a score
That'll leave everyone baffled of your worth.
Thus, if you want to win the game,
Then, let your storehouse of energy feel powerful,
By not setting rules of survival, but in fact revising your dreams and aspirations,
Leaving a lot of scope to breathe easy air,
Going off limits to explore and not to catch the air,
Feeling grounded with peace and meditate positivity,
And not feel pressured like it's schedule for taking pills,
A little pull and push, a fall and gathered strength,
Stress to be the best, keeping aside the beliefs of being least and powerless,
You'll overcome and it'll come with time,
Self-hate to self-care will be easy to define.

Then you stall with a bright smile and tell your
friends and family,
That it was a pleasure to receive a diagnosis from your
mind,
Thanking elements and doctors, hope and pray, to
help you get back on track,
And win the battle with all gag.

And, It's a Wrap!

And, it's a wrap with a saddened heart and teary eyes :') It was a year that not only brought me closer to myself and my dream to be distinctive in the path I have chosen for myself. But a year that brought home a lot of learning, patience and settled peace in times of chaos.

It made me realize that the more people in your vision and behind will work hands down to bring you, your reputation, and your level of motivation down by spreading irrelevant rumours and hushing through closed doors.

It went to a limit where someone in authority that I respected said so demeaning about me, whom I respected through my masters, to people I worked with closing me in the box, making me feel the skills and abilities I had were damaging enough.

I was questioned about having high EQ and CQ by people who termed themselves from the field of mental health. I felt myself going into the cocoon I had built thinking that I am not capable, maybe, I lack everything. I am a failure. While others rode on striving for happiness

—

But not all bad was offered by the Institute of prestige. Soon, in the days that followed, I found my bright shine and platform. I actualised my strength and knowledge. This time I didn't let myself fall out of my will. The new me with intact knowledge and will be stood the times of trials. Soon, the multidisciplinary exposure that the Institute offers, worked to my favour. Everyone realized my true potential and worth. Some amazing people stood next to me, and became my pillars. The conditional was uncovered and the right and truth strived.

—

In the end, the journey I began with was much appreciated and I went to conduct the first few types of research in India in my field of interest. That was called not only unique but stood par the expectations.

—

Today, I feel with the course of time, I could put it out in clear- I know what I am capable of and I'll make the best out of it, always ;)

Section Five

Love, An Expectedly Unexpected Feeling

Before Love

I read it somewhere,
Love is a catalyst to good relationships,
It makes You and I more confinable into we,
But literature got me choked
Filling me with a dilemma of world and cross,
I battled experience of experimentation,
Nothing but hit a bottom rock,
I made love or love made me,
I wasn't sure,
But it definitely took me away from me,
Leaving me deserted and damaged,
Pieces of inner soul scattered on the floor,
Years happened, months passed,
I projected myself to be strong,
Escaping chances and glances of being silent in the chaos,
I told him, I told her, every men and women I met
To stay away from inner demon of love,
Some understood, better than me,
I wasn’t alone on the path, they said
I made love or love made me

I wasn't sure,
But it definitely took me away from me,
Leaving me broken, everytime,
Letting me become an empty vessel with no emotions
Scared to be lonely,
Yet again

A Glass over Love

When more than people,
You rely on glasses
Helping you talk life
with same intention
on a similar frequency
As yours
As, you know you are on path
Path of loneliness or highness
You are challenging unaware about
But, don't belong to the crowd
Crowd, which cheers sameness
A routine to follow, a comfort of stability
For you,
You own a crown,
A crown of difference
And hence merging in,
Demands a glass to go down.

Love, First Dilemma

Still wondering,
Whether it was an added cup to the list or company by my side,
Whether it was singly thinking hundreds of thoughts together or a conversation to share ideals and ideas with,
Whether it was the tea that I felt addicted too, or was it fetching reasons to spend the time together,
Whether it was the time that went by, or it was being transported to an era of looking at time with each passing star,
Whether it was smell of something old being rejoiced or was it lighting of some new candles around the corner?
I wonder!
Deep down in heart with the slurry sip, I knew, I found a home in you.

Establishing Us

Walking through the woods,
Capitalising on the essentials
Avoiding pessimism, leading us
to the land of unknown,

Sitting by the river with canopies of green,
Letting words flow by,
Unravelling in comforts of love and pleasure,
Discovering sides unknown,
Settling down to accept the flaws,

And when by evening winds blow by,
Welcome changes with open hands,
Building a little house of resilience,
Helping us deal with consistencies of ups and downs
with hope and spirit,

Moving on, slowly, from phase to phase
And when withered by sudden storm,
Instead of citing hopelessness and worthlessness,

Let's promise to stand together with head and heart
syncing in strength and courage,
Letting the beauty of variances
influencing us to hold onto,
In the end, keeping a thought alive,
We always have a starry sky to fall back to,
And right in the present moment,

Let us celebrate the goodness and simplicity of new love around the corner in the honest environment of bonfire and tea.

Claiming Love

One early morning on a random day in December,
The sun shone brighter than usual
Everything seemed extremely calm.
It felt like silence before the roar of the storm
Or was it just my clouded imagination after all

It was one of our ordinary meet-ups,
But something seemed different,
It was a day, after a long while,
I felt someone had heard me well
And in return responded me well
He told me things that I always wanted to hear
A feeling which in itself was special

He spoke his words well
Making me dive into deep and swim in confidence.
They, the words, softly fixed themselves
In the wounded, empty holes in my heart
They, the words, were mesmerising in their tone
enough,

They, the words, were calm to put balm on the scars I had got from before,
The troublesome accounts and relationships in the past
They, the words made sense, sounding like a recital of my mother's concerns

I felt robbed from my fears
It reminded me of how I made up stories about tasteless vegetables for my sister
And convinced her to eat, eventually becoming her favourites
It felt unordinary, like how my dad did my hair before sending me to school everyday

He ignited the confidence in me
He made feel enough of myself
He reminded me of boldness that I had
He helped me beat the blabbering mouths of insecurities and demeaning stance
It was like someone was speaking to me,
It was okay to fall and fail sometime
But you can't continue to see the world through dark glasses every time
You have to stand up and take charge
Letting yourself easy and being careless too

I was bewildered with this change,
The feeling was strange yet seemed comforting,
It felt like I was having a conversation with destiny,
And it was her way of spelling that the sufferings of being alone and facing the challenging the world has come to an end,
Time has come down upon you
To be into your stride.

This was simply love, this time.
Letting him in, in my system
Allowing myself into a feeling of being taken care of.

A Long Hug

In the twisted day of romance
It's the feeling of togetherness
Weaving stories about great love
Leaving behind the capacity of thinking of plenty
Because at the end what matters at heart
Stays with you long, like a hug from your loved one

Conflict of Love

It had nothing to deny,
The calmness it held
Was reaching out to both of them,
Who stood there with
Heads lowered, handing in disappointment,
The guilt wrapped them up
And made it impossible
To fetch the light of the promises they made to each other.
They were good friends Infected by love

For each other, they had denied all the time,
Convincing themselves they were
Still in love with their ex- lovers
And they stuck together to fix
The life back for them,
They did activities, sung together
Danced together,
Making world their stage
Without caring for the audience
Their hearts crawled towards each other,

Subtlety pursuing the attention,
The care, the acceptance,
Afraid of these feelings,
Assuming it to be a compromise

In the fire of denied first love,
They started hiding their soul
From each other,
Leaving mere skeletons to interact
Only a spectator could decide,
The love they claimed
They were in,
Was for each other

The past was just an arrangement
Of what felt like love
Instead, was an infatuated friendship
And what felt good and reasonable now
Was a feeling to stay on for years to come ahead,

The wait in the moment was
Unrequited and forced,
A turn around was enough
To feel the said and
Say the emerging feeling

An Indecisive Love Path

Like a dried flower in a notebook
Kept with utmost care
To be looked after
In the memory of someone
Who you longed for or waited for
It can be simply be read as love
For the exchange happened for a reason

Similarly the grey season held me different
Since he left for his voyage
The hope of return was a window closed
I had no option left with me
I was left lifeless
With a black blanket,
I was carrying around to cover my back
Like a dried flower, I laid down on the bed
Longing for my lover to come and take me away
To rise and shine in the waves of superior and inferior
Lands unwatched, unlatching doors that never
opened
To see daffodils dancing to song of the breeze

And stay in a home built with bricks of love and cemented with care
I waited in the ruinous room for long
I took this pain for caressed into love again

Half lit candle stood there every night
To be lit again, to lighten up the dark room
It was time, I would open the book as a routine
And look at the dried flower for hours
Hopelessly waiting for him to come
As he had promised me of his return
And comfort us both, the soul of the flower and half-life human,
It ached hard, unbearably harsh
From the feeling of being unwanted, uncared for

But, it's not easy,
To let go at once
To accept and move on
I guess, it'll take time
For him to turn back and reflect
That someone is sitting in the long rocking chair
Humming his name like a hymn
Waiting to come home
Kiss the life into other human
To be alive again and celebrate love

To the dismay of my anticipation of love
The house of aspiration broke
It got replaced with assembly of actions to stay alone
and alive
I came to a road divided
It was left to me to decide where I wanted to head
next
To a new lover awaiting and life to proclaim love
again
Or to run side by side like a marathon without a
destination
Firing my desire to love yet be loved.

Section Six

A Hope within Chaos

An Ecosystem

I walk a road of basic and highness, where I seek
simplicity and serenity,
I walk a path towards peace and satisfaction internally,
I walk a green bed internalizing that I am grounded,
I walk watching the sky, knowing where balance lies and
limits seemunending.
I walk life meeting opportunities and people, building an
ecosystem ofconcern and an economy of love.

Shadows

Shadows talk,
No, you don't have to quiet to listen to them,
They are possibly communicating all around yourself,
You need to zone in silence and science,
To listen to the real side of human being a human.

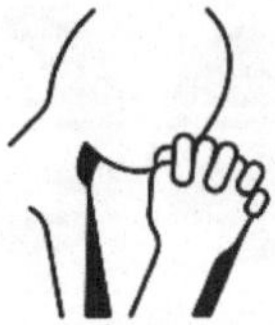

A Decent Prayer

I walk up to you with thousand wishes and hundred words
Hoping even a tenthto be fulfilled,
Satisfying myself with halved happiness and some success,
Running constantly with a million dreams,
Just to be that one in a billion.
Hoping you grant me the permission to make the best of my potential andsupposed opportunity.

Messages for Mr. Thomas Philips

Brethren for Life & Beyond

RW Bro. Thomas Philips, more affectionately known by the name 'Sunny' was more than a friend to me. The bond we shared as brothers will always have a special place in my heart.

Although we often exchanged glances and greetings whenever we crossed paths during the Grand and Region meetings, we first met each other closely in the year 2016 when I become the Founding Member of Lodge Bonhomie No. 435.

A Senior in age; a Senior in Rank; appointed as Secretary of the aforesaid esteemed lodge, had no ego and was one of the most humble and jolly persons I have ever come across. He had an answer for every problem and even though I was younger to him in age, he always addressed me as 'Sir' and often sought my opinion and advice on various issues for masonry and also for non-masonic affairs.

Gradually, the friendship between us began to bloom while discussing and organizing various programmes for our Lodge, including various charity and fundraising programmes, where I came to know of his business and line of work, i.e. 'Printing Press'. He was perfectionist in his work and always carried a humble and professional approach.

During this time, my daughters, Jigyasa and Prerna founded PSY-Fi: For A Healthy Mind, a mental health education organization. For the same, they had started organizing various seminars, conferences, and awareness programmes so as to generate awareness and acceptance of mental health amongst the common public. In the course of these programmes, I connected my daughters with Mr. Thomas so as to handle the printing of their various printable materials, such as posters, banners, certificates, brochures, and magazines, etc. Mr. Thomas participated very proactively and enthusiastically and guided my daughters to prepare and print the finest products for their audiences.

On one such occasion, my daughter, Jigyasa sent him a rough draft of a collection of her poems to get a sample copy of the same to be printed. As soon as the printing was over, I got a call from him indicating that he also had an occasion of going through the collection of Jigyasa's poems and candidly told me that he was really impressed by her thoughts, wisdom, and knowledge. Pressing his authority, he said 'I am keeping one copy of the said book in my Archives to read it over again. Such was the nature of my dear Brother.

This one gesture from his side, sparked a fire in my daughter's heart and since that day, she has worked relentlessly to prepare and compile a version of poems that were dear to her, and those that she wanted to share with the world so that people out there, who had shared similar experiences, resonate with her, and are able to find comfort in familiarity and community.

Sometimes, it is still difficult for me to wrap my head around the fact that he is no longer with us. I vividly remember the last time I met with him in my office, we were supposed to have Tea together, but due to some infection in his throat, he could not have tea that day, and promised me that it will be due for 'next time'. Unfortunately, that Tea party is still due, as he left for the heavenly abode while we were still living in the virtual world because of the pandemic.

However, I'm extremely grateful for having met a great and loving personality like him in this lifetime and I'm thankful for the love and affection he has shown to me and my family in the few years before he left for the heavenly abode.

This love and tribute comes from Jigyasa's own heart as a result of the compassion and confidence shown by him towards her that has given her the strength to publish this collection of books in her own name.

I pay my gratitude to my child for her insight love towards our dear friend.

I, by this note would also like to communicate to the family of my Dear Brother Thomas that we are always available for them 24 x 7.

THOMAS, MY DEAR FRIEND,

I PRAY THAT WHEREVER YOU ARE, YOU HAVE A SMILE ON YOUR FACE AND SPARKLE IN YOUR EYES.

ALWAYS IN OUR HEARTS.

-

- VW Bro. Vivek Kumar Tandon,

Thomas, My Brother, My Friend

I have been asked to pen my thoughts about my dearest brother and friend... And I am so overwhelmed that my thoughts are all jumbled up...I am writing and rewriting...

My memories of him are very happy ones. Even in the most difficult of times I only remember Thomas' in a happy disposition – His ever-smiling face, unflinching faith in the Lord are (sorry, using the past tense for Thomas is something I cannot do because he remains alive in my heart) the hallmarks of Thomas' persona. As I said, my memories are all happy ones...

I remember very vividly the evening when four of our brethren (including R W Bro Thomas) of Lodge Dhanvantari were decorated with the LTS. The enthusiasm of our dear brother was sky-high...all the efforts for organizing and successfully completing the function were of Thomas', including the designing of the momento.

We have had innumerable journeys together on Masonic affairs and otherwise. And Thomas saw to it that they remain etched in our hearts forever.

On the trip to Shimla, when we stayed at the cottage of Bro Vasu Bhasin in Dharampur, under the leadership of R W Bro Sanjay Ahuja.. the lift at Mall was not working and Thomas had to climb up. Thomas was to act as a DOC and was so exhausted that finally, I had played the part.

The last trip that we took together, which included Dr Agrawal, Negiji, Dhawan Saheb and others is so fresh in my mind as though it all happened yesterday. We left Delhi with o plans and prior bookings, and after travelling around 120 km away from Delhi, we started discussing the place of our destination (and this was the month of June when every place is jam-packed) and started our search for accommodation. In the meantime, our dear Thomas bhai makes a few calls and Nainital and Sattal are booked for and we turn our steering wheel to Nainital...what a trip we had ...the cottages at Sattal on the bank of the lake.... The food...everything was just perfect.

A big void remains in our friends' circle after our dear Thomas bhai left for his journey to the heavenly abode. Who will now organise the legendary Christmas Eve parties at Dhanvantari. The parties at his printing press. Oh, what a blast we used to have during Christmas time. Lodge meetings will never be the same without your presence, Thomas bhai.

The press at Karol Bagh was our place for rendezvous. His famous chiding whenever we weren't able to meet for more than 15 days went like "Arrey, Peena chodha hai, par pilaana thodi chodha hai" and "the scotch is waiting for you all" and it still echoes in my heart.

During Corona times our video calls had acquired a certain degree of notoriety...our children had changed their times to make calls knowing that this was the time for brethren...Even when Thomas bhai was in hospital we continued...

I can go on and on...Such is the bond of friendship, of brotherhood. You are missed sorely, my dearest brother and every moment of it...

Rest in peace, dearest brother Thomas Philip

- RW Bro Dinesh Adhlakha

About the Author

Jigyasa Tandon was born and raised in the hustling Capital City, New Delhi in the culturally diverse country, India. Her words and poems are reflective of the distinctive experiences she encounters in her many conversations with people from all walks of life and broadly addresses inherent narratives of human experience.

Hailing from a reputed lawyer family, she chose a divergent path to craft her own life in psychology and mental health education. She is a Trained Mental Health Educator from NIMHANS, Bangalore, and a Counselling Psychologist with expertise in dealing with on-field, grass-roots level, and sensitive groups.

A teacher, motivational speaker, writer, educator, and social worker; her contribution in educating the Indian society about the importance of taking care of one's mental health has been globally recognized and has been instrumental in making her the recipient of the coveted Women Achievers' Award 2021 by the Indian

Achievers' Forum, as well as the prestigious Noam Chomsky Excellence Award in Psychology and Effective Community building for Reformatory Changes in Mental Health and Allied Fields 2021 by the Redpond Educational and Psychological Research Centre, Madurai, India.

She is the Founder of a Mental Health Education Organization by the name of PSY-FI: For a Healthy Mind wherein she has curated unique skill-based programmes and interventions targeted towards India's pressing mental health concerns, such as Suicide Prevention, Adolescents' Mental Health, Depression, Trauma Victim Counselling, Juvenile Delinquent's Rehabilitation, as well as everyday management of mental health difficulties. She has made use of art, writing, theatre, flash mobs, freeze mobs, talk seminars, remedial education projects, media, etc. to communicate the importance of mental health in life.

She strongly believes in the ideology that effective application of psychological principles and life-skills education in can positively contribute in rehabilitation and reformation of criminal offenders, and the same is reflected in her work at various forums of criminal justice system, such as the Tihar Jail (Asia's Largest Jail), Juvenile Justice Board – II, Feroz Shah Kotla; Delhi Legal Aid Services Authority at Patiala House

District Court; Court-appointed Counsellor in various matters concerning women abuse, etc.

She firmly believes that the culture of a society plays a foreground role in understanding the needs, emotions, thoughts, and behaviour of an individual and thus, it is important for every individual to feel belonged and connected to something in life. She cultivates the same in her role as a Teacher and Counsellor at various top schools of Delhi, as well as a resource person and youth mentor for many colleges and forums across India. She has taken up countless lectures, workshops, therapeutic interventions and online programs sensitizing on Mental health awareness, for Advocates, school and college students and teachers, Jail wardens, police officers, and others.

Additionally, she has been in various leadership positions recognizing her sheer will and dedication towards the reformation. She has held prominent positions such as President, Delhi Human Values Council, WICCI 2021-22. She has received special acknowledgement on the Global Youth Education Platform. She was a principal member in organizing India's First and World's Second Walking tour of a Mental Health Institute to deconstruct the idea of mental health treatment – Stories Against Stigma), organized by the Department of Mental Health Education, NIMHANS Bangalore. Moreover, she is the mastermind behind the initiative to bring Spoken Word Poetry and Open Mic Culture in NIMHANS, Bangalore, by the Department of Mental Health Education. She has closely worked on projects as a curator, mentor, and executor with the Department of Mental Health Education, NIMHANS, Bangalore, like Certificate in Mental Health Education, Tobacco Use, Suicide Prevention, Media and Mental Health, and Nursing Training in Mental Health Education, among others.

When not working, she is typically seen in her Indian ethnic attire with a cup of chai, with the notes app of her phone, and indie music playing on her earphones; busy doing something only few can do i.e., creating change.